enjoy Playing the Cello

Margaret Martindale and Robert Cracknell

Note to the Teacher:

The cello is found today in many homes which have not had one before and in many schools which do not have a tradition of string-playing. *ENJOY PLAYING THE CELLO* is a resource of well-known tunes which are arranged so that music notation and a thorough knowledge of unextended first position are gradually introduced.

Fingerings and bowings are given for guidance but are not exclusive. To aid intonation the early pieces have accompaniments for a second cello to be played by the teacher or a more advanced student. In later pieces, the more adventurous may like to improvise simple accompaniments. Some of the tunes have been slightly simplified.

M.M.
R.C.

Music Department
OXFORD UNIVERSITY PRESS
Oxford and New York

CONTENTS

1.	First notes	1
2.	First fingers	3
3.	The A string	6
4.	Sharps (third fingers)	8
5.	Fourth fingers	9
6.	Low notes and quick notes	12
7.	Three in a bar	14
8.	Dots, and some more low notes	16
9.	Second fingers	19
10.	Two in a bar	24
11.	Slurs	27
12.	More slurs, and a new note	29
13.	More dots	35
14.	Off the beat	38

Oxford University Press, Great Clarendon Street, Oxford OX2 6DP
Oxford University Press Inc., 198 Madison Avenue, New York, NY 10016, USA

Oxford is a trade mark of Oxford University Press

© Oxford University Press 1989

No part of this publication may be reproduced, stored in a retrieval system, or transmitted, in any form or by any means, electronic, mechanical, photocopying, recording, or otherwise, without the prior permission of the Publishers.

1 FIRST NOTES

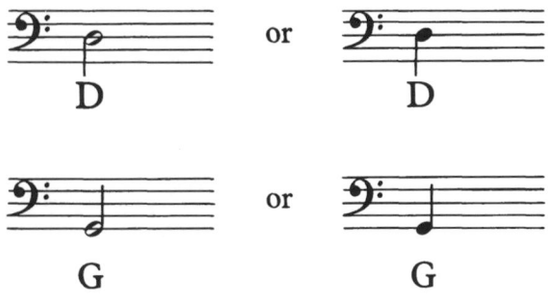

PATTERNS

Nut Tree

Traditional

Any old iron

Charles Collins, F. A. Sheppard,
Fred Terry

Roll out the barrel

Lew Brown, Wladimir A. Timm,
Jaromir Vejuoda

2 FIRST FINGERS

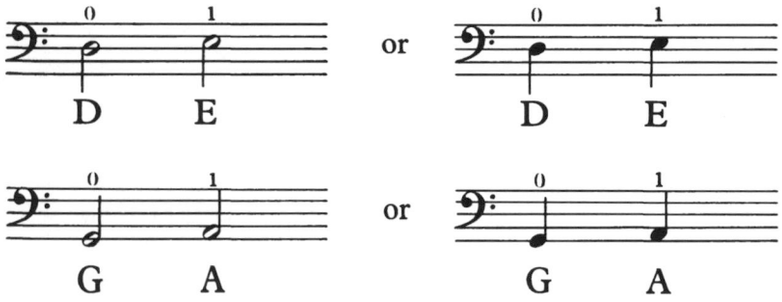

PATTERNS

This old man

Traditional

Michael Finnegan

Traditional

There is a tavern in the town

Cornish Folksong

Yankee Doodle

Traditional

3 THE A STRING

A

A

B

B

PATTERNS

1

2

3

4

William Tell

Gioacchino Rossini
(1792–1868)

Bass

Tune

A Tune by Schubert

Franz Schubert
(1797–1828)

Bass

Tune

Waltzing Matilda

Marie Cowan

On Ilkley Moor

Traditional

4 SHARPS

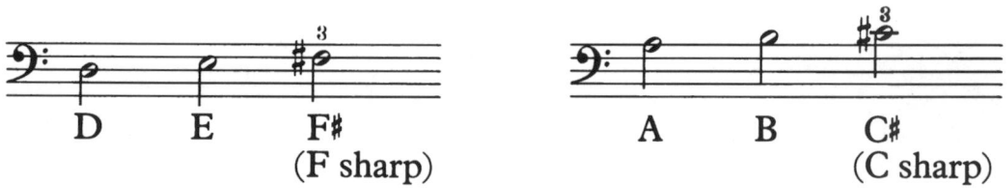

PATTERNS

Hunting song

Traditional

Merrily we roll along

Traditional

Merrily – Again

Traditional

Old MacDonald

Traditional

5 FOURTH FINGERS

G

D

PATTERNS

⊓ = DOWN BOW (Pull) V = UP BOW (Push)

1

2

3

4

TUNES FROM DIFFERENT COUNTRIES

Holland – Carol

Traditional

France – au clair de la lune

Traditional

* Originally: 

Hungary – Folk song

Traditional

Russia – Folk dance

Traditional

America – Aunt Rhody

Traditional

6 LOW NOTES AND QUICK NOTES

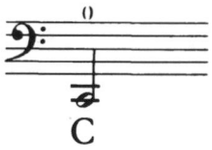

PATTERNS

1

2

3

The Drunken Sailor

Sea shanty

Tom Dooley

Traditional American

Camptown Races

Stephen Foster (1826–64)

Lulu

Billy Rose, Lew Brown,
Ray Henderson

7 THREE IN A BAR

PATTERNS

Blow the man down

Sea shanty

London's burning

Traditional

Oh, dear! What can the matter be?

Old English song

Morning has broken

Traditional

Ludwig

Drink to me only with thine eyes

Traditional

8 DOTS, AND SOME MORE LOW NOTES

Michael, row the boat ashore

Spiritual

Kookaburra's Song

Traditional

Greensleeves

Traditional

Puff, the magic dragon

Peter Yarrow

* Originally: 

Can-Can

Jacques Offenbach (1819–80)

Frère Jacques

Traditional

Augustin

Traditional

Cockles and mussels

Traditional Irish

9 SECOND FINGERS

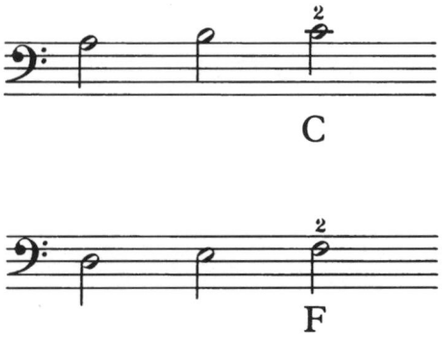

PATTERNS

Supercalifragilisticexpialidocious

Richard M. Sherman,
Robert B. Sherman

John Peel

Traditional

Villikins

Traditional

Red River Valley

Traditional American

Lilliburlero

Traditional

My old man's a dustman

Lonnie Donegan

St. Anthony Chorale

Traditional

TUNES TO PLAY, USING 2nd AND 3rd FINGERS

Early one morning

Traditional

Sucking Cider

Based on 'The Lone Fish Ball'

Daisy, Daisy

Traditional

The Ash Grove

Traditional

Polly-Wolly-Doodle

Traditional

The Yellow Rose of Texas

Traditional

Skip to my Lou

Traditional

10 TWO IN A BAR

PATTERNS

Nuts in May

Traditional

The Farmer's in his den

Traditional

Yankee Doodle

Traditional

Oats, Peas, Beans

Traditional

Short'nin' Bread

American work song

Dargason

Traditional

Farandole

Georges Bizet (1838–75)

Nelly the elephant

Ralph Butler, Peter Hart

German folk-song

Traditional

The Teddy Bears' Picnic

John W. Bratton
James B. Kennedy

11 SLURS

PATTERNS

1

2

3

4

Alouette

Traditional

My Grandfather's clock

Henry C. Work

Country Gardens

Traditional

The Vicar of Bray

17th century

The Quartermaster's Stores

Traditional

Flow gently, sweet Afton

Traditional

12 MORE SLURS, AND A NEW NOTE

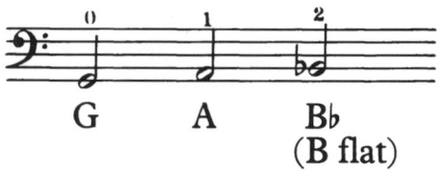

PATTERNS

1

2

3

4

London Bridge

Traditional

Polly, put the kettle on

Traditional

Golden Slumbers

Traditional

Cradle Song

Johannes Brahms (1833 – 97)

Largo

Antonin Dvořák (1841–1904)

Looby Loo

Traditional

Rule Britannia

Thomas Arne (1710–78)

Parade of the Tin Soldiers

Léon Jessell

MORE TUNES TO PLAY

Hornpipe

Traditional

Rakes of Mallow

Traditional

Jimmy crack corn

Traditional

The British Grenadiers

Traditional

Pack up your troubles

Felix Powell

Tune from 'The Nutcracker'

Peter Tchaikovsky (1840–93)

Barbara Allen

Traditional

Oh! Susanna

Traditional

The Elephant

Camille Saint-Saëns (1835–1921)

13 MORE DOTS

PATTERNS

1

2

3

A-rovin

Traditional

Kum-ba-ya

Spiritual

Show me the way to go home

Irving King

Notice that 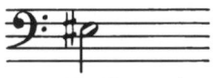 is played with the same finger as 

(E sharp) (F natural)

John Brown's body

Traditional

Poor Old Joe

Stephen Foster (1826–64)

Loch Lomond

Traditional Scottish

Clementine

Traditional

A Tune by Mozart

Wolfgang Mozart (1756–91)

She'll be coming round the mountain

Traditional

14 OFF THE BEAT

PATTERNS

Round and round the village

Traditional

Nobody knows

Traditional

Mocking Bird

Traditional

Swanee River

Stephen Foster (1826–64)

Swing low, sweet chariot

Spiritual

Jamaica farewell

Traditional

The Sloop John B.

Traditional

DANCE DUETS

Waltz – Roses from the South

Johann Strauss II (1825–99)

Ragtime

Mátyás Seiber (1905–60)

Gavotte

Johann Sebastian Bach
(1685–1750)

Clarinet Quintet Minuet

Wolfgang Mozart (1756–91)

Samba – Mango Walk

Traditional

Song of the King (Rock)

Music: Andrew Lloyd Webber
Lyrics: Tim Rice

Printed in England by Caligraving Limited Thetford Norfolk

INDEX

Alouette 27
Any old iron 2
A-rovin' 35
Ash Grove, The 23
Au clair de la lune 10
Augustin 18
Aunt Rhody 11
Barbara Allen 34
Blow the man down 14
British Grenadiers, The 33
Camptown Races 13
Can-can 18
Carol 10
Clarinet Quintet Minuet 43
Clementine 37
Cockles and mussels 18
Country Gardens 28
Cradle Song 30
Daisy, Daisy 22
Dargason 25
Drink to me only 15
Drunken Sailor, The 12
Early one morning 22
Elephant, The 34
Farandole 25
Farmer's in his den, The 24
Flow gently, sweet Afton 28
Frère Jacques 18
Gavotte 42
German folk song 26
Golden Slumbers 30
Greensleeves 17
Hornpipe 32
Hungarian folk-song 11
Hunting song 8
Jamaica farewell 40
Jimmy crack corn 32
John Brown's body 36
John Peel 20
Kookaburra's Song, The 17
Kum-ba-ya 36
Largo 30
Lilliburlero 21
Loch Lomond 37
London Bridge 29
London's burning 14
Looby Loo 31
Ludwig 15
Lulu 13
Merrily we roll along 8
Michael Finnegan 4
Michael row the boat ashore 17
Mocking Bird 39
Morning has broken 15
My Grandfather's clock 27
My old man's a dustman 21
Nelly the Elephant 26
Nobody knows 39
Nutcracker, The 33
Nuts in May 24
Nut Tree 1
Oats, Peas, Beans 25
Oh Dear! What can the matter be? 15
Oh Susanna 34
Old Macdonald 8
On Ilkley Moor 7
Pack up your troubles 33
Parade of the Tin Soldiers 31
Polly put the kettle on 30
Polly-Wolly-Doodle 23
Poor Old Joe 36
Puff (the magic dragon) 17
Quartermaster's Stores, The 28
Ragtime 42
Rakes of Mallow 32
Red River Valley 20
Roll out the Barrel 2
Round and round the village 38
Rule Britannia 31
Russian folk dance 11
Samba-Mango Walk 44
St Anthony Chorale 21
She'll be coming round the mountain 37
Short'nin' Bread 25
Show me the way to go home 36
Skip to my Lou 23
Sloop John B 40
Song of the King (Rock) 45
Sucking Cider 22
Supercalifragilisticexpialidocious 19
Swanee River 39
Swing low, sweet chariot 40
Teddy Bears' Picnic, The 26
There is a tavern in the town 4
This old man 3
Tom Dooley 13
Tune by Mozart, A 37
Tune by Schubert, A 6
Vicar of Bray, The 28
Villikins 20
Waltz—Roses from the South 41
Waltzing Matilda 7
William Tell 6
Yankee Doodle 5
Yankee Doodle (two in a bar) 25
Yellow Rose of Texas 23